Guess What

Published in the United States of America by
Cherry Lake Publishing
Ann Arbor, Michigan
www.cherrylakepublishing.com

Content Adviser: Susan Heinrichs Gray
Reading Adviser: Marla Conn, ReadAbility, Inc.
Book Designer: Felicia Macheske

Photo Credits: © Protasov AN/Shutterstock Images, cover; © Gallinago_media/Shutterstock Images, 1; © schankz/Shutterstock Images, © 3, 9; Patricia Chumillas/Shutterstock Images, © 4; bjonesphotography/Shutterstock Images, © 7; Destinys Agent/Shutterstock Images, © 10; nico99/Shutterstock Images, © 13; Seregraff/Shutterstock Images, © 14; Evgeniy Ayupov/Shutterstock Images, © 17; Annette Shaff/Shutterstock Images, 18; © Andrey_Kuzmin/Shutterstock Images, back cover; © Eric Isselee/Shutterstock Images, 21, back cover

Library of Congress Cataloging-in-Publication Data

Macheske, Felicia, author.
 Lanky legs / Felicia Macheske.
 pages cm. — (Guess what)
 Summary: "Young children are natural problem solvers and always looking for answers, especially when it involves interesting insects. Guess What: Lanky Legs: Praying Mantis provides young curious readers with striking visual clues and simply written hints. Using the photos and text, readers rely on visual literacy skills, reading, and reasoning as they solve the insect mystery. Clearly written facts give readers a deeper understanding of how the praying mantis lives. Additional text features, including a glossary and an index, help students locate information and learn new words"— Provided by publisher.
 Audience: K to grade 3.
 Includes index.
 ISBN 978-1-63470-720-6 (hardcover) — ISBN 978-1-63470-750-3 (pbk.) — ISBN 978-1-63470-735-0 (pdf) — ISBN 978-1-63470-765-7 (ebook)
 1. Praying mantis—Juvenile literature. 2. Children's questions and answers. I. Title.
 QL505.9.M35M33 2016
 595.7'27—dc23
 2015026087

Cherry Lake Publishing would like to acknowledge the work of The Partnership for 21st Century Skills.
Please visit *www.p21.org* for more information.

Printed in the United States of America
Corporate Graphics

Table of Contents

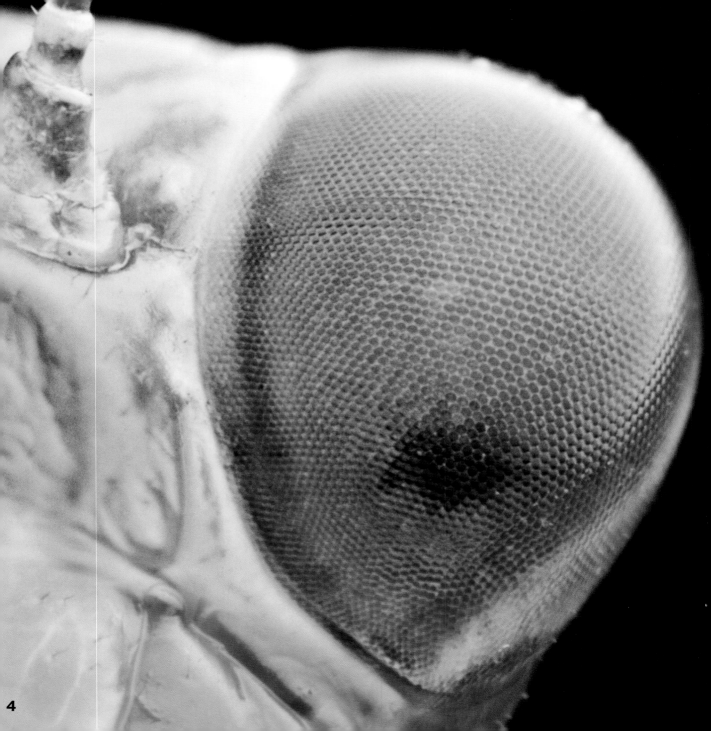

4

I have very big eyes to look for food.

Sometimes I can change color to hide.

I catch food with my long front legs.

9

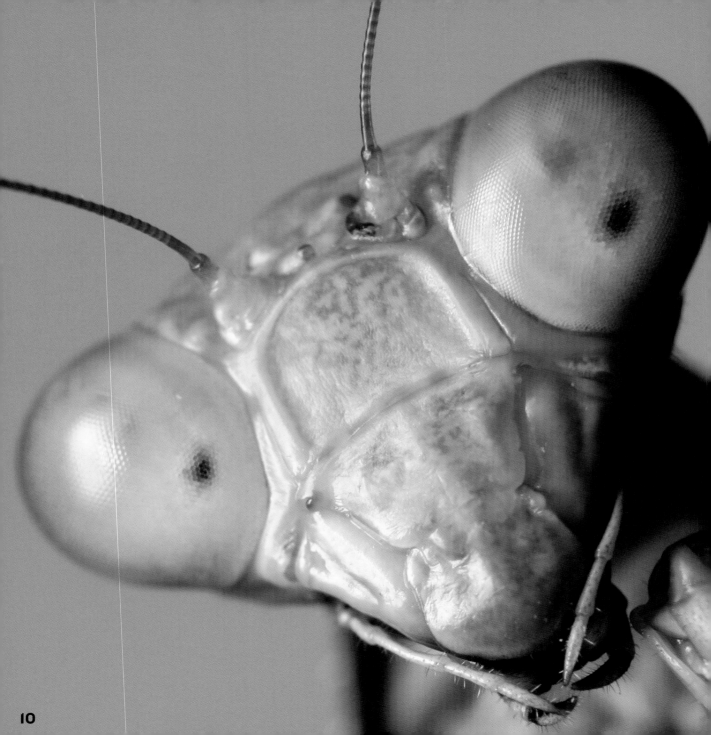

My head is shaped like a triangle.

Sometimes I like to dance.

14

I might lay
hundreds
of eggs
in a case.

I need to molt so I can grow.

17

Yum!

I like to eat other insects.

Do you know what I am?

I'm a Praying Mantis!

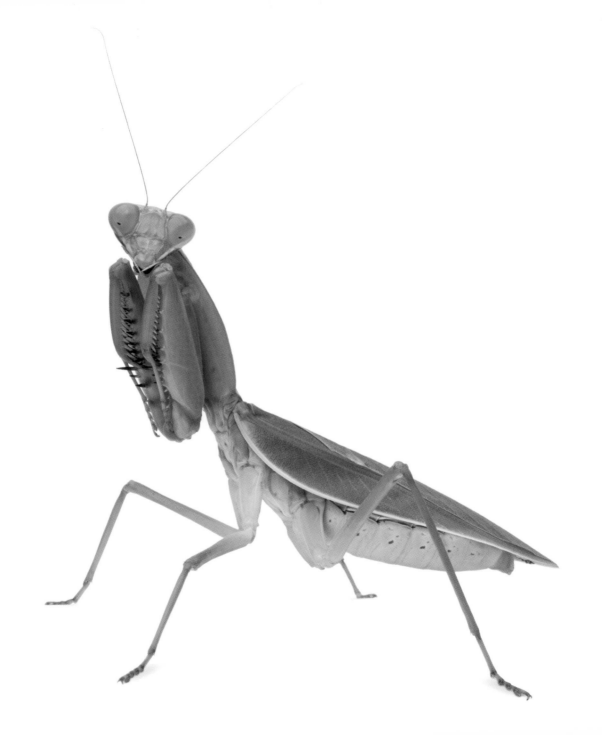

About Praying Mantises

1. A praying mantis sometimes eats another praying mantis.

2. Praying mantises have five eyes.

3. Praying mantises have only one ear. It is located on their belly.

4. A newborn praying mantis, or **nymph**, looks like a tiny adult praying mantis.

5. Praying mantises can turn their heads 180 degrees. That means they can look straight behind themselves.

Glossary

case (KASE) an object that is used to hold something

insects (IN-sekts) small animals with no backbone, six legs, and three main body sections

molt (MOHLT) to break out of old skin or an old shell, in order to grow larger

nymph (NIMF) a name used for some insects, such as praying mantises, that have not yet become adults

Index